DATE			
Kristy T7			
JAN 11	✦		
Pitcher			
Hasketh			
Schrade			
Herbert			
B			
SEP 2 9 1994			
FEB 1 2 1996			
MAR 03 '89			
K K			
SEP 2 2 1995			

CORN IS MAIZE
The Gift of the Indians

Popcorn, corn on the cob, cornbread—and corncob pipes! Tacos and tamales and tortillas! All these and many other good things come from an amazing plant that the Indians discovered and taught the white man how to grow.

In her own magical way, Aliki tells the story of corn: how Indian farmers thousands of years ago found and nourished a wild grass plant and made it an important part of their lives, how they learned the best ways to grow and store and use its fat yellow kernels, how they shared this knowledge with the new settlers of America.

Cheerful illustrations by the author complete this lively account of the Indians' gift to us all.

For Alicia, John, Darius, and Noel

CORN IS MAIZE
The Gift of the Indians

written and illustrated by
ALIKI

Thomas Y. Crowell Company · New York

LET'S-READ-AND-FIND-OUT SCIENCE BOOKS

Editors: DR. ROMA GANS, Professor Emeritus of Childhood Education, Teachers College, Columbia University
DR. FRANKLYN M. BRANLEY, Astronomer Emeritus and former Chairman of The American Museum–Hayden Planetarium

LIVING THINGS: PLANTS

Corn Is Maize: The Gift of the Indians
Down Come the Leaves
How a Seed Grows
Mushrooms and Molds
Plants in Winter
Redwoods Are the Tallest Trees in the World
Roots Are Food Finders
Seeds by Wind and Water
The Sunlit Sea
A Tree Is a Plant
Water Plants
Where Does Your Garden Grow?

LIVING THINGS: ANIMALS, BIRDS, FISH, INSECTS, ETC.

Animals in Winter
Bats in the Dark
Bees and Beelines
Big Tracks, Little Tracks
Birds at Night
Birds Eat and Eat and Eat
Bird Talk
The Blue Whale
Camels: Ships of the Desert
Cockroaches: Here, There, and Everywhere
Corals
Ducks Don't Get Wet
The Eels' Strange Journey
The Emperor Penguins
Fireflies in the Night
Giraffes at Home
Green Grass and White Milk
Green Turtle Mysteries
Hummingbirds in the Garden
Hungry Sharks
It's Nesting Time
Ladybug, Ladybug, Fly Away Home
Little Dinosaurs and Early Birds
The Long-Lost Coelacanth and Other Living Fossils
The March of the Lemmings
My Daddy Longlegs
My Visit to the Dinosaurs
Opossum
Sandpipers
Shells Are Skeletons
Shrimps
Spider Silk
Spring Peepers
Starfish
Twist, Wiggle, and Squirm: A Book About Earthworms
Watch Honeybees with Me
What I Like About Toads
Why Frogs Are Wet
Wild and Woolly Mammoths

THE HUMAN BODY

A Baby Starts to Grow
Before You Were a Baby
A Drop of Blood
Fat and Skinny
Find Out by Touching
Follow Your Nose
Hear Your Heart
How Many Teeth?
How You Talk
In the Night
Look at Your Eyes*
My Five Senses
My Hands
The Skeleton Inside You
Sleep Is for Everyone
Straight Hair, Curly Hair*
Use Your Brain
What Happens to a Hamburger
Your Skin and Mine*

And other books on AIR, WATER, AND WEATHER; THE EARTH AND ITS COMPOSITION; ASTRONOMY AND SPACE; and MATTER AND ENERGY

*Available in Spanish

Copyright © 1976 by Aliki Brandenberg

Library of Congress Cataloging in Publication Data   Aliki.   Corn is maize.   SUMMARY: A simple description of how corn was discovered and used by the Indians and how it came to be an important food throughout the world.   1. Maize–Juv. lit.   2. Indians–Food–Juvenile literature.   [1. Corn]   I. Title.   SB191.M2A584   633'.15'09   75-6928   ISBN 0-690-00975-5   (LB)

3   4   5   6   7   8   9   10

CORN IS MAIZE
The Gift of the Indians

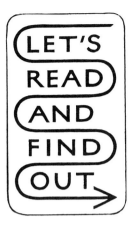

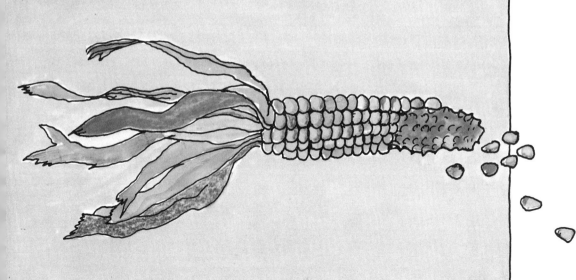

This is a kernel of corn.
It is a corn seed.

Kernels of corn are planted in a small hill of good earth.

The sun shines down on them.

Spring rains water the soil.

The hard seeds soften and sprout.

1

A leaf appears
and a stalk
begins to grow.

More leaves
come from joints
called nodes.

A corn stalk
shoots up fast.
Farmers say that
on a quiet evening
they can hear
the corn growing.

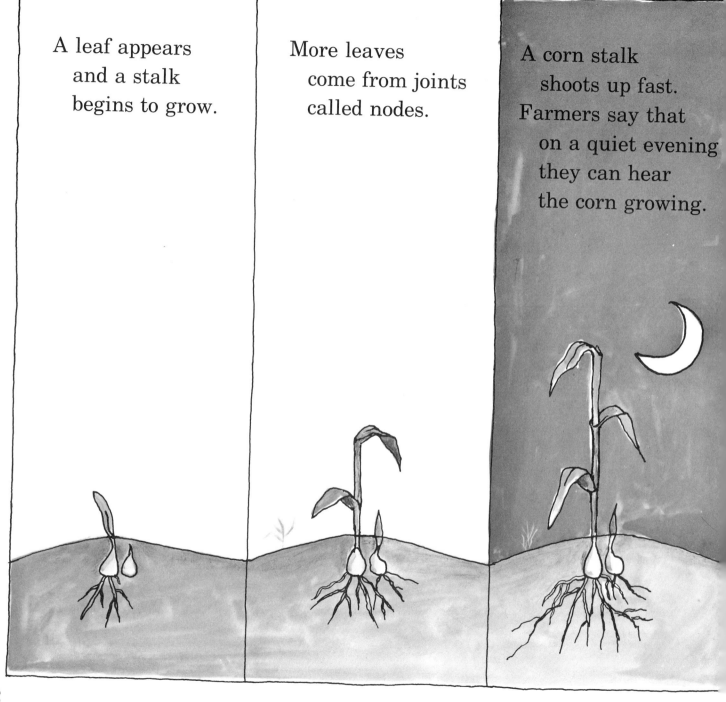

By midsummer, the plant is taller than a farmer.
Husks have begun to sprout from the nodes.
A husk is a bundle of leaves tightly wrapped
around strands of silk.

The corn silk is the female part of the plant.
Tassels grow like a hat at the top of the stalk.
The tassels are the male flowers.

In the summer breeze, clouds of tiny grains
  of pollen blow from the tassels.
The pollen falls on the silk of neighboring corn plants.
Each pollen grain pollinates the strand of silk it sticks to.
After fertilization, a kernel of corn will grow at the
  end of each strand.

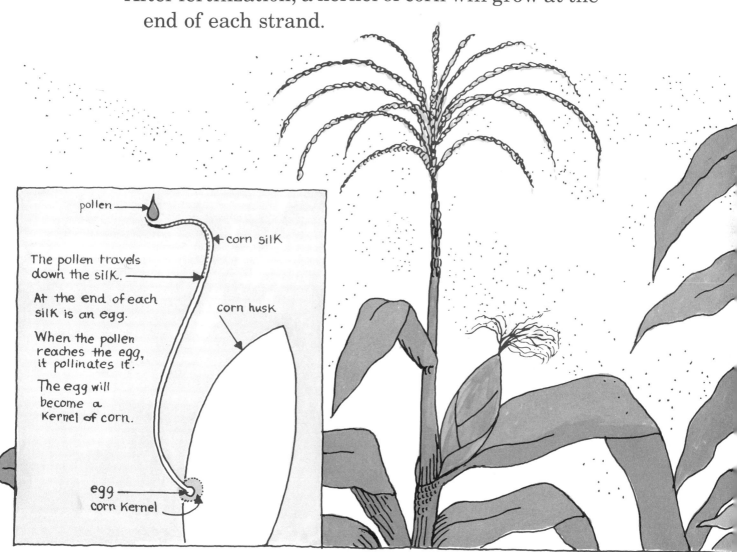

pollen

corn silk

The pollen travels down the silk.

At the end of each silk is an egg.

When the pollen reaches the egg, it pollinates it.

The egg will become a kernel of corn.

corn husk

egg
corn kernel

The corn husk grows.
Inside the wrapped leaves, hundreds of
kernels grow into an ear of corn.
The silk turns from a creamy color to
dark red to brown.

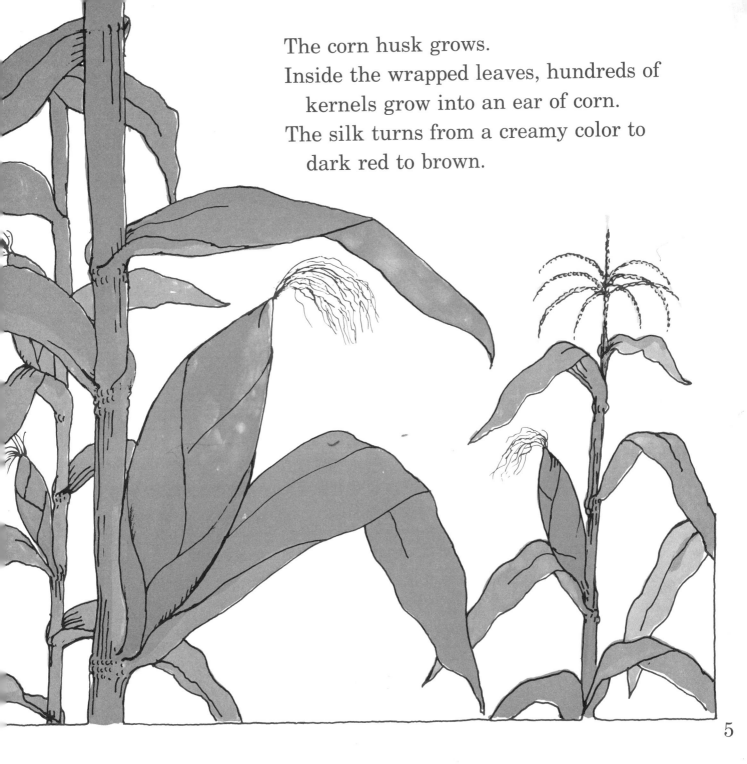

Just before it turns brown, it is time to pick
the corn and husk it.
The husks and the silk are pulled away.
The sweet, juicy ear of corn is ready
to cook and eat.

Farmers leave some ears on the stalk.
The brown silk dries.
The kernels harden and are saved.
They are seeds for the next crop.

Many plants can grow wild.
The wind scatters their seeds over
the earth and they can grow.

Corn kernels cannot fly off the ear
and scatter.
If an ear fell to the ground, a sprout
would grow from each kernel.
The new sprouts would grow in a
tangled heap and die.

Corn cannot grow by itself.
Corn seeds must be planted so there is space around
each hill for the tall plants to grow.
The plants must be weeded or the baby sprouts
will be choked.
Corn cannot grow without the help of man.

Then where did corn come from?
How did it start?
For many years there was no answer.
It was a mystery.

Scientists knew corn belongs to the same
  grain family as wheat, rye, oats, barley, and rice.
They are all grass plants.
They all have jointed stems and nodes.
They all grow wild.
But although scientists searched, they had
  never found any wild corn.

wheat

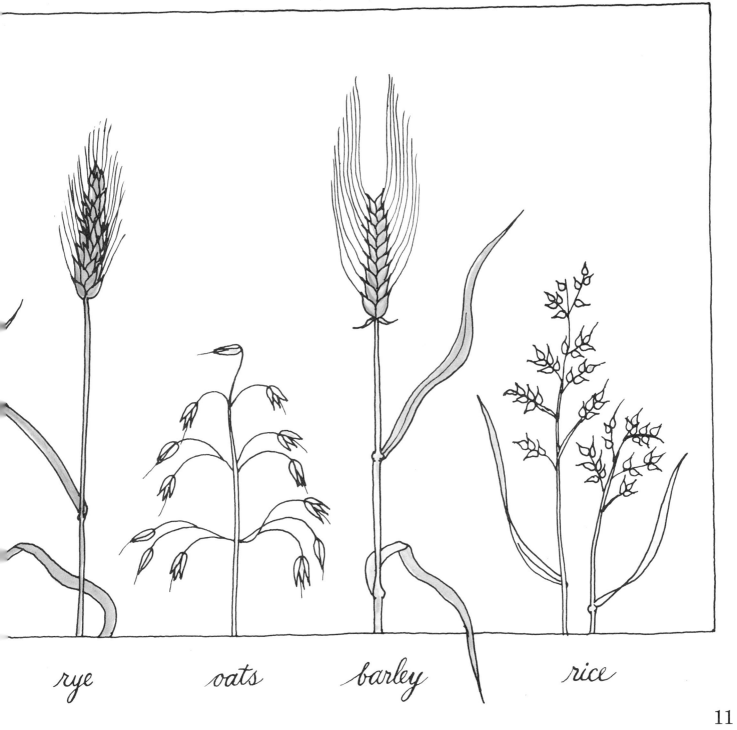

rye   oats   barley   rice

Not long ago they found some.
It was in a cave in Mexico where people once lived.
They found scraps of plants and tiny ears of
    ancient corn, more than 5,000 years old.
It was not like any the scientists had ever seen.

At last they could piece together the story of
    how corn began.

Thousands of years ago, people lived in caves
    in South and Central America.
They planted the seeds of a wild grass,
    perhaps one found in the cave.

Teosinte growing wild.

Scientists think the ancient plant was a tall stalk
  with one ear at the top.
The tassel grew out of the ear.
Each tiny orange or brown kernel was wrapped in
  its own husk or pod.
The kernels grew so loosely they could fall off the
  cob and plant themselves.
The cave dwellers planted and cared for this pod corn.

In time, some scientists think, the pollen of
  another grass, called teosinte, or pollen of other
  plants, fertilized the corn.
It took hundreds of years for the plants to grow
  stronger and the ears larger.

Pollen of other plants and teosinte mixed with pod corn to make bigger and bigger ears of corn.

People found the grain was good for them.
It made them stronger than just beans, squash,
    and other plants they knew about.

Tribes in the north began to grow corn, too.
In time, people in all the Americas were growing
    different kinds.
They learned the right time to plant according
    to their climate.

Different tribes planted in different ways.
Some tribes planted five seeds in a hill.
Others planted two.
Some tribes planted bean seeds with the corn
    kernels so the vine could grow up the stalk.
Many tribes learned to bury a fish in each hill.
The fish rotted and made good soil.

By the time Christopher Columbus landed in the New World,
  the people he named "Indians" were expert farmers.
The women tended the crops while the men hunted.
They harvested the corn.
Some of it they ate fresh.
Most of it they dried.
They saved some for seed.
The rest they ground into meal on a
  flat stone called a metate.
They ate the meal dry or made bread with it.
They cooked it into mush.

19

Indians of Mexico used cornmeal to make pancakes
    called tortillas.
They made tamales by wrapping spiced meat
    mixed with meal in husks and boiling them.

Many tribes boiled tiny, tender corn in the husks
    and ate the ears whole.
They ate corn on the cob.
They popped it.

Tribes in the north cooked corn with beans and
    called it misickquatash.
Indians ate the tassels of the corn plant and
    sucked the sweet, fresh stalks.

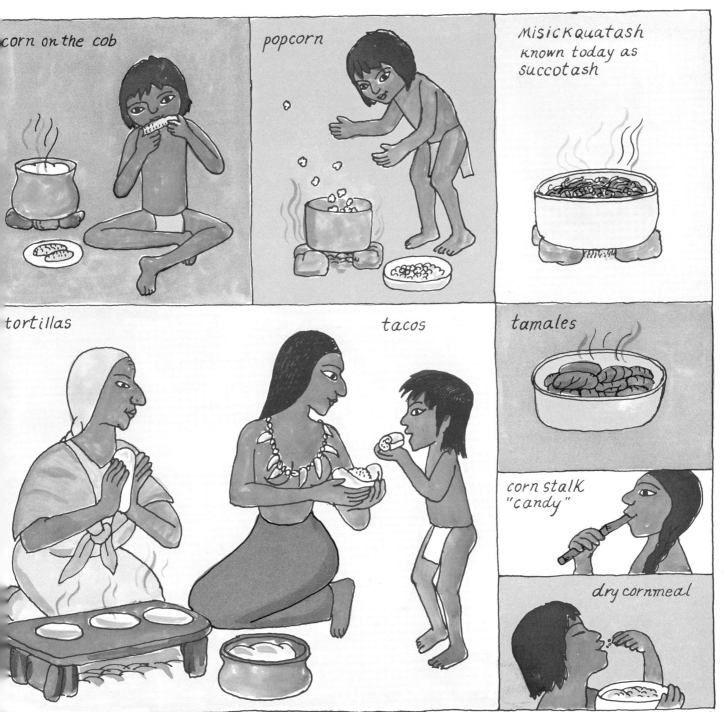

corn on the cob

popcorn

misickquatash
known today as
succotash

tortillas

tacos

tamales

corn stalk "candy"

dry cornmeal

21

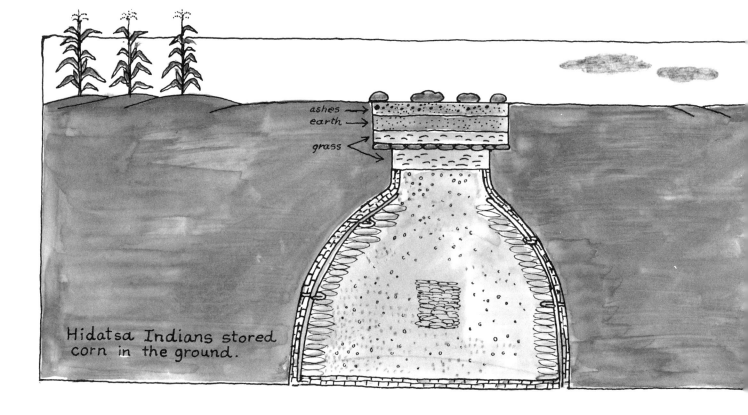

ashes →
earth →
grass →

Hidatsa Indians stored
corn in the ground.

They learned to store corn for the
   long winter ahead.
Corn, the Indians' only grain, was their main food.
Their lives depended on it.
Corn was so important to them, the various tribes
   prayed to the Corn Gods they believed had
   sent it to them.

Some Ancient Corn Gods

23

They had festivals at planting time and at harvest.
They chanted and made music, and each tribe
danced its own Corn Dance.

Pueblo Corn Dance
of today

When Christopher Columbus returned to
    Europe he told of the Indians
    and the grain they grew.
He called it maize, which sounded
    like the name the Indians had used.
Even today the correct word for
    corn is maize.

The word "corn" means "grain."
Corn is also the word used for
    the most important grain a
    country grows.
In some countries wheat is called
    corn.
In others, oats are called corn.
The Pilgrims called maize
    "Indian corn," and Americans
    have called it corn ever since.

Christopher Columbus

Maize

Different Kinds of Corn

When the Pilgrims landed in America, maize saved
their lives.
Indians gave them the dried grain to eat and
showed them how to plant the crop.

On the first Thanksgiving, the Pilgrims and the
Indians together gave thanks for the corn
harvest, as the Indians had done long before.

The Pilgrims learned other things from the Indians.
They stuffed mattresses with husks, burned cobs for fuel,

made corncob pipes and corn-shuck dolls, too.

Today people all over the world grow corn.
There are many, many kinds.

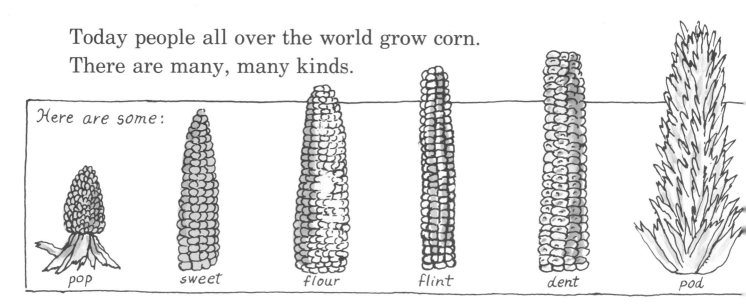

Here are some:

pop sweet flour flint dent pod

We eat only sweet corn, and use popcorn for popping.
The rest is used to feed animals and to make:

corn flour cornmeal cornstarch corn oil corn syrup cereal

baby powder glue soap alcohol medicine .. and many other things.

Now scientists have developed new kinds of corn
   that have more and better protein than any other kind.

People need protein to make them strong and healthy.
Scientists hope someday this new corn will
   help many hungry people in the world.

Harvester

On large farms today machines help farmers plow
and sow seeds.
A harvester picks corn and dries it so it can be
stored without rotting.
Then it is taken to a mill to be ground.

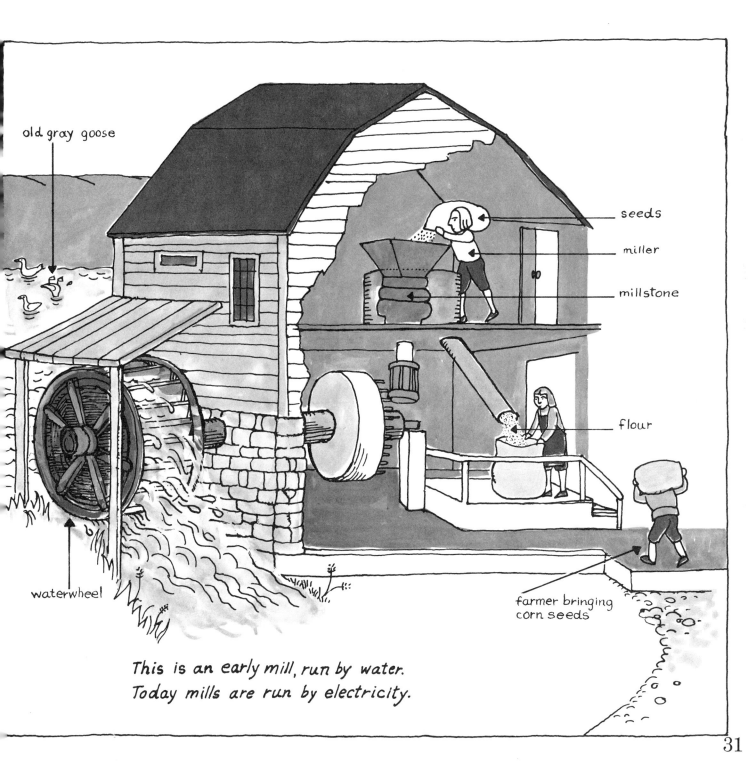

old gray goose

seeds

miller

millstone

flour

waterwheel

farmer bringing
corn seeds

This is an early mill, run by water.
Today mills are run by electricity.

31

But not all corn is planted and ground by machines.
In parts of America, Indian farmers still grow their corn.
They plant the seeds as their ancestors once did.
They care for the plant, harvest it, and grind
  it on a metate.

And they praise the corn that has fed
their people for thousands of years.

ALIKI'S CORN HUSK DOLL

ABOUT THE AUTHOR-ILLUSTRATOR

Aliki Brandenberg has been fascinated by corn ever since she took her first bite and felt the butter drip down her arm. She also has a great interest in American Indians, their culture and art. In this book, both subjects are brought together.

Mrs. Brandenberg often treats her family to corn fritters, corn bread, and other corn dishes. Then, being a person who throws nothing away, she makes dolls and wreaths with the husks.

Aliki grew up in Philadelphia and was graduated from the Philadelphia College of Art. She now lives in New York with her husband and two children in the winter, and spends summers in Switzerland and Greece and other countries where corn grows.

ALIKI'S CORN HUSK WREATH

1. Bend a wire hanger.

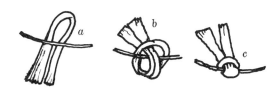

2. Fold one fresh husk (a) and tie it over hanger (b and c). Repeat and repeat. When wire is full—

3. —use pin to shred. Let it dry.

4. Finished wreath.